THE HIGH SOCIETY

What Happened When The Country Finally Went To Pot

An Informal Chronicle by

MORT GERBERG

For Bob Abel, who cares about what he does and
for Judith, who cares . . .

Special thanks to Michael Johnston for his wonderful
assistance in making this new edition a reality.

Barking Hollow Studios, Inc.
www.barkinghollow.com

NEW EDITION! First Published in 1973, But Speaking the Same Truths to Today's Society!

Introduction By Mort Gerberg

One of the prevalent characteristics of the turbulent, society-changing 1960s was marijuana. It was seemingly ubiquitous, though usually covert because it was illegal — which only made it more attractive as a contemporary "subject," on the lips of many, so to speak — and therefore perfect material for humor.

I drew single-panel "pot" cartoons and shopped them to both small and mass-market magazines, figuring that at least all editors would be liberal-minded. I was surprised, however, when one of them, very tall, stood up during our meeting at the *Saturday Evening Post* in 1963, stretched his arm over his head, extracted a joint from one of the tiny holes in a ceiling panel, and lit up. A few weeks later, the *Post* published my cartoon, which caused some controversy, of a hippie looking into his window box and saying, "*It must really be Spring, Sheila; the marijuana plant is blooming.*"

Then, in 1966, as the use and celebrity of marijuana use increased, I created a cartoon spread called "The Junkie Battalion," that *The Realist* published, without controversy. It was inspired by a news story reporting a bill, introduced by a Republican congressman, to draft "punks" with criminal narcotics records and create "junkie battalions."

My (cartooning) interest in marijuana heightened in 1972 when a *Newsweek* magazine story speculated that legalization was imminent. I considered drawing another cartoon spread, but my "what-if" ideas kept spreading, and resulted in this 158-page satire, which, when I reread it last year, looked like a rough draft for the legalization movement that's now growing nationwide.

The first pages of "The High Society" reprise actual reports about marijuana use, Richard Nixon's war on permissiveness and the work of the National Organization For The Reform of Marijuana Laws, the marijuana lobby (founded in 1970 by *Playboy* Magazine). Then it spins into scenarios that spoof special interest groups, shameless commercialism and grabby politics, among others, while using different genres, such as cartoons, scripts, short stories and other narratives.

Now, in 2018, it's still mostly illegal, but the marijuana industry is growing like a cash-crop weed. Nine states plus The District of Columbia allow it for recreation and 30 allow it for medicinal use. Other states are lining up for legalization; cannabis is a big-business industry, having harvested almost $9 billion in sales in 2017, and predicting $21 billion in 2021!

And I find it amusing — a turn-on — to see how my 40-year-old, wacky, predictive imaginings in this book are now playing in real life; virtually becoming today's news headlines.

Rothberg

Viewed in retrospect, the Government's legalization of marijuana undoubtedly had the most telling effect on the nation of any event during the post-Watergate-Nixonian years.

The very day after the Pot Bill was signed into law, for example, the entire country was shaken by an epidemic of hiccups, brought on by involuntary gulping.

What had once been a pipe dream was suddenly a reality that was momentarily hard to swallow.

However, in recalling the events leading up to Legalization, everything can be seen as part of a very logical progression. In the simple terms of the old cliché, Legalization was an Idea Whose Time Had Come . . .

I. The Road to Legalization

The basic idea of legalizing marijuana was hardly new; the old NEWSWEEK Magazine had done a cover story on the possibilities as far back as September, 1970.

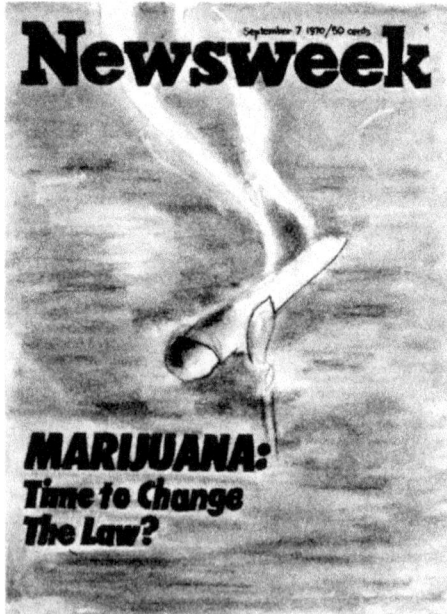

Newsweek

September 7 1970/50 cents

MARIJUANA:
Time to Change
The Law?

And in March, 1972, during the first Nixon Administration, the President's own Commission on Marijuana and Drug Abuse actually recommended a policy of decriminalization, suggesting that penalties for its use be lightened. Considering the preceding years of the harshest legal and moral condemnation of marijuana, this report was nearly tantamount to official sanction.

Accompanying signs of liberalism were appearing from all sides. In November, 1972, William F. Buckley, Jr., the voluble conservative editor-journalist, advocated removing criminal penalties for the use of marijuana. Mr. Buckley even admitted to having smoked a joint himself on his yacht (outside the three-mile limit, to keep it legal).

He would, he said, lend the weight of his magazine, THE NATIONAL REVIEW, to revise the country's anti-pot laws. If the conservative Mr. Buckley favored liberalizing the marijuana laws, wrote THE NEW YORK TIMES, can the country be that far behind?

Apparently it was not, according to the results of a Gallup Poll, reported in February, 1973. The study showed a marked *increase* in the number of people who had tried marijuana (up from four percent to twelve percent in three years) and a definite *decrease* in those who opposed its legalization. Other surveys indicated an even greater escalation of marijuana use dating exactly from President Nixon's second inauguration, especially in Massachusetts and in Washington, D.C. This increase was explained by a noted therapist writing in PSYCHOLOGY TODAY as the "hysteria-anxiety-desire by political liberals (as well as the man in the street) to avoid the pain and frustration of 'four more years.'"

But despite this apparently warming liberal tilt toward marijuana, the cold fact was that the second Nixon Administration launched itself with a declared "War on Permissiveness" in America. This comprised attacks on crime, pornography, abortions, the press, children's education, the poor, social rehabilitation, the mentally retarded, sexual fulfillment, the aged, and all nay-sayers who in the eyes of the Nixonians, definitely included marijuana users.

"Guess what? Creamed spinach has just been put
on the permissiveness list."

Mr. Nixon personally rejected his own Drug Commission's recommendations for decriminalizing marijuana, and set the tone for cracking down on permissiveness. He spoke patronizingly of "the average American" as a child, saying that if "you pamper him and cater to him too much, you are going to make him soft, spoiled and . . . very weak . . ." An official position such as this was quickly interpreted as an open invitation for increased control and manipulation of the public by Big Business, the lawmakers and other vested-interest groups. So, in combating permissiveness in the "interest of national security," a restrictive, repressive atmosphere clouded the nation, whereby marijuana users continued to be officially regarded as depraved criminals, and dealt with most severely.

However, during the same period, a number of pot-lobbying groups formed and proved to be effective in changing minor individual state laws. Most were small, very special-interest groups, like Mommas For Marijuana, Poppas For Pot, Grannies For Grass and Jocks For Joints — organizations which achieved good results, but which were limited in scope and influence.

The most important of all the pot lobbies was the National Organization For The Reform Of Marijuana Law (NORML), under the leadership of a young activist-lawyer named Ron Norton. NORML was extremely successful in advancing the marijuana-law-reform movement, acting as spokesman, center of information and legal arm. Within a few years, the lobby had established offices in 55 cities, enlisted thousands of volunteer organizers and had made its presence known to hundreds of reform-minded local and state legislators.

However, when NORML's influence finally began to be noticed on Capitol Hill, the Administration became uneasy and moved to undermine the group's efforts. In one characteristic tactic, pressure was brought on foundations, like PLAYBOY Magazine, which had contributed heavily to the lobby.

"Let me put it this way, Mr. Hefner — unless you cease and desist from sponsoring the activities of NORML, we shall, by means of a new, creative interpretation of the Interstate Commerce Laws, enjoin you from pushing tits and snatch."

This oblique approach failed, however, and the Nixon Administration followed with a civil suit that the WASHINGTON POST called "irresponsible overkill, designed obviously to crush the entire marijuana movement in one devastating attack." Mr. Nixon apparently also hoped that this controversial action would make the country finally forget the Watergate shame, the disgrace of Spiro Agnew, Presidential income taxes, and the countless other government level manipulations and scandals identified with him at that point in time.

In specifying the conspiracy charges brought by the Government against NORML, the Attorney General, who had named himself as one of the plaintiffs, claimed that the actions of the lobby "in attempting to promote, produce and foster an unholy atmosphere of national degradation and permissiveness through the encouragement of the promulgation and use of the . . . vile weed . . . effectively constituted a personal violation of my civil rights."

As Government blunders go, wrote TIME Magazine, this suit was "a blunderbust." The trial continued for months, constantly making front-page news with bizarre courtroom "happenings" arising from the direct examination of marijuana. Witnesses, for example, were asked to testify twice, once before turning on and then after smoking the "vile weed." The liberal press produced colorful reports about the trial which captured everyone's imagination and nudged public opinion toward the positive percentage side on the pot issue.

It was then, while the defense was in the middle of presenting its case in court, that President Nixon appeared on prime-time television to deliver his memorable "Checkered State of the Mind" speech. A major portion of that speech, it may be remembered, consisted of Mr. Nixon reading, emotionally, from a slim, little-known tome entitled, "Indian Hemp. A Social Menace," written by an English lawyer and published in London in, 1952, in which, among other things, marijuana is referred to as "the killer drug" and the "narcotic poison" which "always causes a very marked mental deterioration and sometimes produces insanity." Hence, marijuana is frequently called "loco weed," the book stated. "*Loco* is the Spanish word for 'crazy'," the President explained confidentially during his televised talk. Mr. Nixon went on to select and read passages, apparently at random and out of context.

"And listen to this, and I quote from page 30: 'the majority of investigators . . . believe that marijuana smoking is widespread among school children . . .' and here, '. . . juvenile delinquency is directly related to the effects of the drug; that it is a causative factor in a large percentage of our major crimes and sexual offenses; and that physical and mental deterioration are the direct result of the prolonged habit of smoking marijuana.'"

"Marijuana smoking is usually done in places called 'tea pads.' Listen, and I quote from page 35: 'A tea-pad is a room . . . in which people gather to smoke marijuana. The majority of such places are located in . . . [um-um] Harlem . . . the [um] landlord, agent . . . [um] the janitor is aware of the purposes for which the premises are rented' . . . and just listen to this part, my fellow Middle Americans . . . 'the walls are frequently decorated with pictures of nude subjects suggestive of perverted sexual practices.' Excuse me, my friends, but I will not bring any more of this material into the sanctity of your living rooms and/or dens. . . ."

After a moment where he visibly struggled to control his emotions, Mr. Nixon went on to speak about marijuana as the

cornerstoned [sic] of a permissive society and characterized those who advocate marijuana as the "architects of permissiveness." He said he regarded them as criminals upon whom he could not "drape the forgiving cloak of amnesty."

Said Mr. Nixon, "Now, with regard to the question of amnesty for those who have chosen to associate themselves with, and further perpetuate permissiveness of this nature, let me simply say this. Certainly I have sympathy for any individual who has made a mistake. We all have made mistakes. But also, it is a rule of life, we all have to pay for our mistakes . . . now as far as amnesty is concerned, I have stated my views, and those views remain exactly the same . . . amnesty means forgiveness. Now, let me make this perfectly clear. We cannot provide forgiveness for those people who wallowed in the permissiveness of marijuana. Those people who deserted the morality of this country for their own morality must pay their price, and the price is not a junket in the Government employ or something like that . . . the price is a criminal penalty . . . (I would not even rule out the possibility of excommunication) . . . for disobeying the laws of the United States."

Mr. Nixon concluded his telecast by showing a short film entitled, "Reefer Madness," a 1936 Government-made classic which links marijuana to murder, prostitution and madness. Mr. Nixon was apparently unaware that the very same film was currently being shown by NORML, as part of its fund-raising programs, to dramatize the origins of antiquated Government thinking.

Mr. Nixon's startling interruption of the NORML trial notwithstanding—the White House press secretary later stated that it was all a coincidence, that "the President had simply made another courageous decision to speak out for the good and welfare of the American people and that he had had no idea that such a suit was actually taking place"— the jury voted unanimously for complete acquittal, after smelling pot smoke drifting from the judge's chambers.

The exoneration of NORML was a great victory for the advocates of marijuana, and the grass-rooted consciousness was raised to a new high. There seemed to be more people smoking and more people willing to admit it. Also relevant was the fact that the greatest increase of marijuana use was registered in Middle America. The "new majority," which had been the principal force in developing a conservative political tone in the country, seemed now to be leaning toward liberalism, at least as far as pot was concerned. After the heavily restrictive, anti-permissive climate of the Nixon years, Middle America was restive and looking at life with a more open mind. The Nixon days were by this time numbered, and the new candidates and politicians were campaigning on much more liberal platforms. Perhaps, thought Mr. and Mrs. Middle America, marijuana was *not* an evil. Maybe it was even fun.

These subtle changes in attitude were not lost on the American tobacco lobby. Since the publication of the Surgeon General's original reports linking cigarette smoking to lung cancer, and the subsequent Federal restrictions on advertising, the tobacco manufacturers had been among the strongest foes of marijuana legalization. The industry had feared the huge, competitive threat which marijuana represented.

With Richard M. Nixon finally out of power, replaced by a more liberal-platformed President and Administration, and the clear switches in public opinion about marijuana, the tobacco lobby swung 180 degrees the other way, reversing its stand. The thinking was sublime in its American purity: If you can't fight 'em, join 'em; but better still, take over. And so the vast power of the American tobacco lobby began pressuring Congress for Legalization.

At this point the drug industry jumped in, having been doing some profitable thinking of its own, and proclaimed its endorsement and active support of the tobacco industry's reform movement. Legalization would enable the drug manufacturers to develop their own pot products and cash in on the millions of people who were interested in turning on but resisted smoking; those who had kicked the cigarette habit or those who were afraid of starting.

And so, supported by the combined influence of two of the most powerful industry lobbies in the country, and promising the Government a brand new source of tax revenue amounting to possibly $3 billion a year, the legalization of marijuana was quickly a solid bet in Washington.

Naturally, there was some opposition, notably from the liquor industry, which stood to lose an enormous amount of business. Also, there were a few opposing special-interest groups, like the DAPS (Drunks Anti-Pot Society), and the Highway Lobby, which was apprehensive of a cutback in Federal funds for more road-building because they were afraid people would be less likely to need public roads if they tended to go off on private trips, and the trial-lawyers associations, which were still carrying on a fight against no-fault insurance. But the pot bandwagon had become a steamroller, and was not to be stopped. The Marijuana Legalization Bill (H.R. #28463) was introduced to Congress and met its only strong opposition in a filibuster attempt by a few moonshine-drinking Southern Dixiecrats.

"... the drinker and the drug addict are
worlds apart ... even alcoholism, for all its
occasional ... um ... discomforts and
inconveniences ... does not usually poison one's
nature ... but drug addiction does. How seldom
we use the expression, 'alcohol fiend,'
but the phrase, 'drug fiend' comes to the tongue
more quickly and easily ... and so I say
to you my fellow legislators, that if God
had intended Man to turn on, then He would
have created Man with a switch. ..."

The filibuster ended when its leaders passed out, and the bill was approved by an overwhelming majority in both Houses and signed the next day by the new President.

After years of illicitness, suddenly marijuana was legal. Just like that. Congress had seen the light.

II. Reactions of the Authorities

The law enforcement officials and authority figures unquestionably experienced greater difficulty than other people in adjusting to the new legal status of pot. For years the police, politicians, district attorneys, clergymen, judges and other community leaders had been applauded for their efforts in persecuting pot smokers. But Legalization ended all that and abruptly forced these people to re-examine their basic attitudes on the subject. Some, unable to change with the times, decided to continue, privately, fanatically, a war against marijuana, even though that, ironically, was now illegal.

> The most well-known case on record was of Lt. Richard L. Cook of the Chicago Narcotics Division. Lt. Cook had pursued marijuana smokers with such relentless, dedicated fervor that he became known as the Pot Broiler. For Lt. Cook, the enactment of Legalization signaled the termination of his *raison d'etre,* the very end of his life as he had known it.
>
> The conflicted man's mind snapped. He would wander through the streets of Chicago, day and night, carrying a blue laundry bag, picking up cigarette butts and placing them under arrest.

Lt. Cook, or the Mad Potter, as he was later called by police psychiatrists, was retired from the police force on half-pay and made an honorary member of the Sanitation Department.

Most of the country's authority figures, though, decided to adapt, and accept marijuana. Many were secretly delighted by Legalization because it freed them to publicly express attitudes about pot which they had kept private for many years.

(One politician from Kentucky, who had been a powerful weapon/spokesman in ex-President Nixon's war on permissiveness, overnight became one of marijuana's most ardent supporters. However, as it was subsequently revealed during the controversial "Cigarette Papers" Senate Investigation, the politician had been a longtime secret stockholder in four tobacco companies, and during the same period that he was opposing pot for Nixon, he was secretly contributing to research for the commercialization of marijuana.)

There were many others from all levels of law and/or order who eagerly welcomed Legalization, for although it might create other problems, they felt, at least it brought fast relief from a certain hypocrisy.

*"Well, I, for one, **always** thought it was better than creme de cocoa...."*

"It kills me just to **think** about it! All those raids hundreds and hundreds of pounds of confiscated pot! But did we ever **save** any of it? Oh, **no**—not **us!** . . ."

"All these years I was admiring Senator Abel's
unwavering attention span; now it turns out
he's just been stoned all the time."

"I finally understand, Chris, why you find religion so uplifting."

"*Poor Cinnamon. She really had become quite fond of marijuana-detection duty.*"

III. Reactions of the Media

The media wasted little time in mining the riches of the Legalization story. Newspapers, magazines, television, radio, publishing, films, all rushed to report or explain, feature and dramatize the new sensibility. The news weeklies ran in-depth cover stories; the newspapers did continuing series; magazines offered special features, like GOOD HOUSEKEEPING's "Preparing Your First Pot Party"; the "Dear Abby" column offered advice on whether or not it was proper etiquette for a gentleman to offer a lady a joint on the street; TIME, Inc. began publishing a new magazine called HIGH LIFE. There was something for everyone.

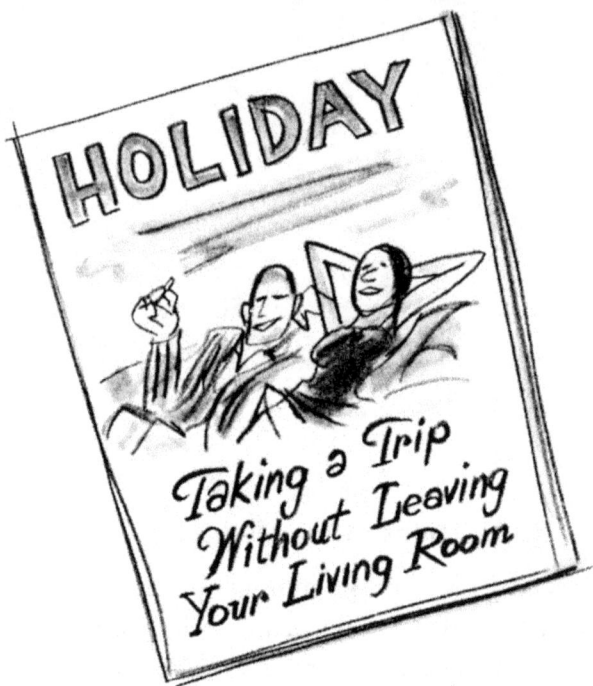

HOLIDAY

Taking a Trip Without Leaving Your Living Room

PLA...

potma
of th
mon

COSMOPOLITAN

THE ULTIMATE INTIMACY:
SHARING HIS JOINT.

SPECIAL 32 PAGE PULLOUT SECTION

TURNING
ON
190 FEET
UNDER
THE
INDIAN
OCEAN

Pot in Every One

"Good evening. Well, the news from here
doesn't look too bad—not too bad at all...."

"How about this, Avery—Boy Meets Girl!
They turn on! Pow! Skyrockets! Love, love,
love! They come down. Bleh! Feh!
Boy **Loses** Girl! He pursues her! They turn
on! Pow! Love, love, love!
Boy **Gets** Girl! **Fadeout!**"

"Remember, though—when the cookies are done,
you're supposed to eat them, not smoke them."

*"Bob! We just got a sure-fire bestseller!
An updated version of 'Leaves of Grass!'"*

The most sensational and controversial media development, however, was credited to the syndicated Washington columnist, Jack Anderson. Anderson had speculated how "incredible" it seemed that only a few days after the enactment of Legalization, the first commercially produced and packaged marijuana cigarettes, a brand named Cheshirefeels, was distributed to retail outlets across the country. Even the "good old American know-how" answer couldn't satisfy the question of how it was done so fast.

Anderson pursued the story. His investigative reporting soon provoked a Congressional hearing which produced a body of information that became known as "The Cigarette Papers." The Cigarette Papers revealed how the leaders of the tobacco and cigarette industry had met secretly during the early days of the second Nixon Administration. They anticipated then that their greatest future profits could be reaped from commercialized marijuana and, accordingly, they created an elaborate master plan to realize that end. While they openly sought to curry favor and avoid conflict with the Nixon Government by fighting marijuana law reform, they conducted another, totally different, secret life.

As it was revealed at the hearings, a huge laboratory/factory was constructed in the deepest bowels of a hidden section of Mammoth Cave in Kentucky. There, brought in and isolated from the rest of the world, hundreds of men and women lived and worked to solve the problems of mass producing marijuana; of growing it, manufacturing cigarettes, distributing, marketing and advertising them. In short, there was created, covertly, underground, a major new American industry as big as natural gas.

"What's new in the underground? I could tell you
what's new, but you'd never believe it."

"Damn your tan, Sherick!
This is a plantation—not a beach!"

"I see where Jerry worked overtime again."

*"Who says a high-efficiency assembly line
has to be dull?"*

"Hiyah, honey—haven't we met before, someplace?
The Manhattan Project? Cape Canaveral? Yalta? . . ."

The Mammoth Cave Project was conceded to be a superbly run operation, conducted under the tightest security conditions. Its secrecy was dramatized through testimony of the workers, who indicated that they never really knew where they were and after regularly smoking Cheshirefeels cared even less about knowing.

Q: Now, Mr. Daniel, please look at this slide and tell the committee what you see.

A: I asked you before, Senator, call me "Mole."

Q: Sorry, I forgot. If you please, then, Mr. Mole—

A: No "Mister." Just "Mole." Down in the hole . . . is the Mole . . . playing a role? . . . searching his soul? . . . seeking a goal? . . .

Q: Uh—excuse me—Mole

A: . . . digging for coal . . . like a troll . . . taking his toll . . .

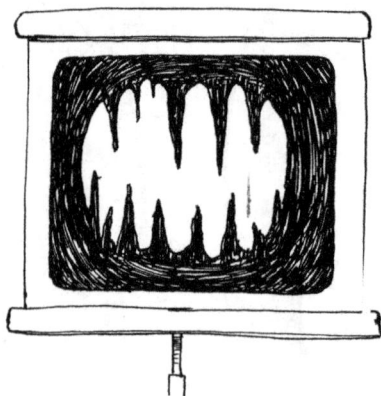

Q: Mole! Please, the slide! What do you see?

A: Oh—uh, nothing—it's too bright. Wait'll I put on my shades, here—OK—uh—now that place there looks like the entrance to one of the caves we worked in.

Q: The entrance into one of the caves, you say?

A: Well, don't quote me; it could also be an entrance out.

Q: Mr.—uh, Mole, you have told us, under oath, may I remind you, that you were a foreman in the research section. How is it that you cannot be sure of where this photograph was taken?

A: 'Cause it was always dark, man! I mean, like, they always kept us in the dark, you get what I mean?

Q: Tell us.

A: Well, like just being there. I mean, I'm really an actor. The only reason I went to the cave in the first place is because they told me it was an audition for that new Tom Sawyer movie.

Q: In the cave?

A: Sure, you know; Tom—the cave—Becky—Injun Joe—like that.

Q: And so?

A: So I was held over.

Q: For a few years?

A: Well, you know, a gig is a gig. Excuse me, but after looking at it again, I think you got that slide in upside down.

Q: I do?

A: Yeah, its the stalagmites that go up and the stalactites that go down, and the way you have it there, you got the stalactites going up and the stalagmites going down. That's why I was confused.

Q: But how can you tell the difference?

A: Listen, man, you spend enough time with them, you can tell.

According to the testimony, the research had proceeded at full speed, nonstop. It was made clear, through the statements of several witnesses, that the cigarette lobby had only been waiting for the entire commercial operation to be developed before it officially reversed its position and came out in favor of Legalization.

There were references to a number of mysterious exchanges of money and covert meetings between the cigarette groups and certain people in the previous (Nixon) Administration. There was, ultimately, the question of the timing of the introduction to Congress of the Legalization Bill itself, which corresponded almost exactly to the first production target date of Cheshirefeels. Unfortunately for the investigation, the production schedule memo which would have corroborated all the allegations had been shredded.

To accusations that he and his group had exerted "uncommon influence on the Government of the United States and its representatives to further (its) own ends," Mr. Raleigh Winnston II,

chairman of the Association of Cigarette Manufacturers, and longtime presidential confidant, replied that it was "merely the American way" and that this "business operation" was actually an "excellent manifestation of the admirable Nixonian era of self-determinism . . . a natural outgrowth of the pioneer spirit which made frontier America strong and great."

The investigation also raised an interesting but never fully answered question of how it had been possible, during the Nixon years of widespread Government wiretapping, bugging, spying and surveillance, for private industry to build and maintain the Mammoth Cave Project without the Government's knowledge, as it claimed.

The Senate committee sought to call White House aides to testify, but former President Nixon invoked what he called the "well established precedent" of "ex-post-facto-a-priori executive privilege," not only for himself, his family, his friends and his colleagues, but also anyone who ever talked football with him. The Supreme Court—now all Nixon appointees—granted him the absolute immunity he sought and that part of the investigation was dropped.

The Cigarette Papers Investigation ended with all principal figures being legally exonerated from any wrongdoing, although a certain moral censure was insinuated. This added an intriguing, romantic appeal to marijuana and all its advocates. Raleigh Winnston II, emerging as the most dominant figure in commercial marijuana, was heavily sought after by the media. Magazines continually published feature articles about him. Winnston seemed to encourage them, appearing wherever there was a reporter and photographer. His name was constantly in the newspapers and he became a regular on the late night television talk shows, extolling marijuana with considerable restraint and dignity, especially considering the approaches taken by many of his interviewers.

"Tell me now, Mr. Winnston—and you can give it to me straight all right—all right, just watch it out there—um, is it really true what they say about—well, you know—about the—uh—sexual powers of pot?"

"Well, Johnny, I'm not really sure what you mean by 'what they say.'"

"Oh, c'mon, Raleigh, you know what I mean—eh? —like does pot put more lead in your pencil?—eh—more pow in your pod?—I mean when you—or anybody, for that matter—after all, we don't have to get all that personal here—when a guy turns on, is there more joy in his joint? In a manner of speaking, naturally—eh?"

"Let me just put it another way, Johnny. Marijuana certainly does raise one's enjoyment level."

"Heck, I thought it raised a lot more than that."

At the same time, another figure entered the public consciousness, one much more low-key, but certainly of at least equal importance to the Legalization story. This was Ron Norton, the young activist lawyer who had been the driving force of NORML, the National Organization for the Reform of Marijuana Law. Norton had never been a public figure, preferring a certain anonymity for his crusading work. During the Cigarette Papers Investigation, however, Norton became prominent when he testified, although somewhat reluctantly, to Winnston's "public-spirited attitude" in advancing commercial marijuana.

Norton, who philosophically opposed Winnston's methods and principles, admitted that he agreed to help defend him

only because in the early days of the Legalization movement, Winnston had contributed a good deal of money to NORML for its public education campaigns. There were several articles written about Norton, his sincerity and his dedication, but he never excited the public imagination the way Winnston did.

Raleigh Winnston II and Ron Norton were interesting subjects, but for the media there were many possible angles to explore in the Legalization story. It had a rich past to recount; there was the present, with the continuing developments of new commercial applications of marijuana; and there was the future, with its promise of countless variations.

IV. The Products

Within three months of the President's signature on the Legalization Bill, the pot business was bubbling over. Thanks to the years of secret research in Mammoth Cave, the entire marijuana cigarette operation, from planting to distribution,

was running like a fine Swiss watch. The Association of Cigarette Manufacturers, under the smooth Winnston, had sliced the pot pie into five main companies: Cheshirefeels, Real Cools, Oldogoldos, Mah-Boos and Djust Djoints (purposely spelled with a "d" to avoid litigation on the matter of using generic terms).

The cigarettes were manufactured and packaged in regular assembly lines. They came filtered, non-filtered, with and without menthol and were rated upwards in strength from one Z to ten Z's, the Z referring to the old cartoon symbol of being asleep, according to the press releases. (According to the public, on the other hand, the Z stood for "zonked.") The milder cigarettes produced a slow glow; the stronger ones gave the smoker a super-accelerated high. The cigarettes were sold in packs of ten or twenty, but were also initially sold like cigars, to be bought one or two at a time, appealing to those with carry-over feelings for the old way. Cheshirefeels and Mah-Boos were priced a bit higher, to attract the "better clientele," and Djust Djoints were priced the lowest, for the working class.

"A packet of Cheshirefeels, my good
man—anna packa Djoints."

Every market was covered from coast to coast. Marijuana cigarettes were distributed at cigarette counters, in machines, wherever regular tobacco was sold; although it did feel a bit strange at first to be able to buy a joint in the same candy store where you would usually get a chocolate malted, or in the supermarket next to a rack of READERS DIGESTs.

Not only were the cigarette companies boasting of booming business, the drug companies were also cashing in happily. Although joints were legal, there were millions of people who had heeded the old Surgeon General's warning and had quit smoking, and hundreds of thousands of others who had never started. But their desire to turn on with marijuana could just as easily be satisfied by drug products.

The prospect of a brand new $100 million-a-year product line was the reason that the drug lobby had eagerly supported and campaigned for Legalization. So, soon after packaged marijuana cigarettes appeared on the market, drug stores across the country began selling without the need of a prescription, such items as pot inhalers and nasal sprays (used as you would an antihistamine to clear your head); the very popular Potstilles, which were small, cherry flavored sucking candies which you kept under your tongue, and by the time they dissolved, so had all your tensions; or Marijuana-nated Chewing Gum, which came in spearmint, doublemint and triplemint, and suggested that you "chew, chew, chew your troubles away" . . . among others.

"Yeah, but what did you do with the dirty books?"

"Oh, its much better than any **chemically** produced tranquilizer, madam. This contains **cannabis sativa**—Mother Nature's own magic ingredient."

*"I don't care what kind. I just want
fast, Fast, FAST relief!"*

The great success with marijuana enjoyed by the cigarette and drug companies, combined with all the publicity and press coverage, assured the *total* commercialization of pot. Certainly the psychedelic influence had already been important to the pop culture of the late Sixties and early Seventies, but under Legalization it became the dominant theme. Every product or service even remotely connected with marijuana was redesigned and remarketed to take profitable advantage of the new mode, and though there were a number of new products developed, most of the new marijuana-motivated business was in the area of creative packaging and promotion.

"... among the key colors in our line will be
Panama Red, Grass Green, Acapulco Gold,
Ultra Oregano and Hash Brown...."

"Perhaps you'd like to get him our new marijuana model—it comes with a safety belt, to keep him from flying too high."

"This one is absolutely guaranteed to turn him on—it has the fragrance of a burning joint."

"Coffee, tea or grass?"

"Well, it only takes 20 minutes—but it seems like two hours."

V. Advertising and Marijuana

The advertising and marketing community was naturally elated over Legalization because of the potfuls of new profits it promised. New products always breed new promotion campaigns and, as TIME Magazine wrote, "The advertising agencies were breeding hard, indeed."

On radio, on television (the old Federal ban on cigarette advertising somehow did not apply to joints), in print and displays, there was a constant barrage of ads and commercials singing the praises of marijuana. Many of the first ad campaigns were suspiciously derivative, at the very least, but nobody complained. In the early days of commercial marijuana, *really* effective advertising was not very important. According to one business columnist, "the beauty part of the new products" was that they only needed "a very soft, sweet-smelling sell."

*"Ah **always** suck Potsies b' fore goin' out on th' field. They he' p me relax and keep mah mahynd offa gettin' hurt. Sheet, man, ah' d **nevah** play this murderous game without fuhst bein' a little crazy in th' head. . . ."*

Things Go Better With Pot

® A JOINT PROMOTION with COKE

Come to the HIGH Country ...

Smoke Mah-boo

"Ole! It looks like El Exigente likes our crop!"

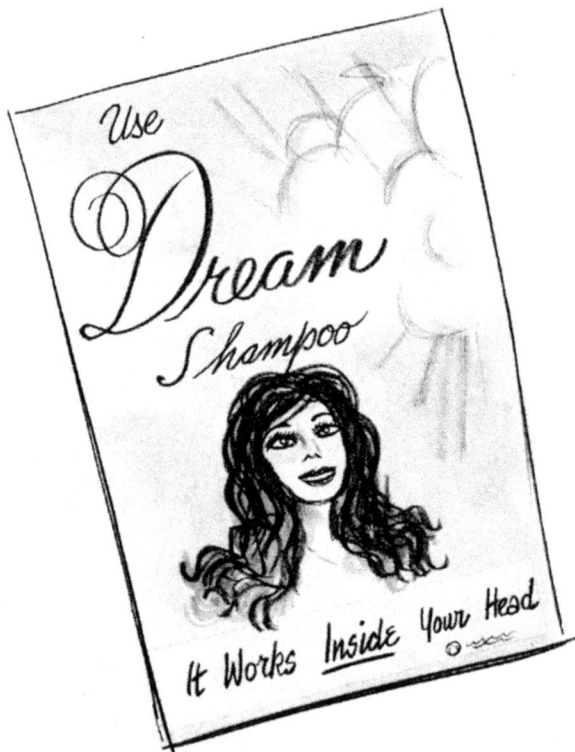

Use *Dream* Shampoo

It Works <u>Inside</u> Your Head

"Since I started brushing with Hypana, I've had
23 percent less cavities . . . and those I **do**
have, I just don't worry about."

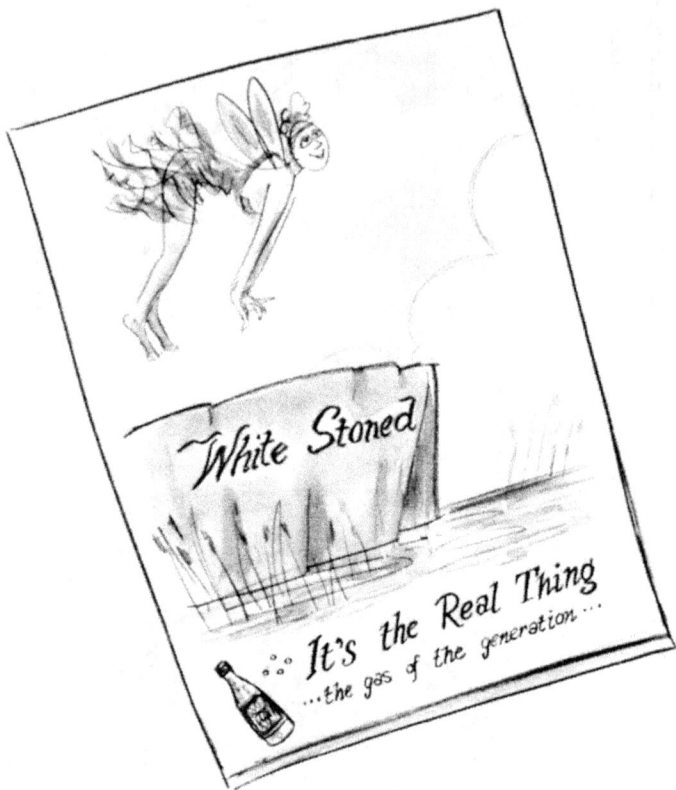

After the first joyful consumer rush, though, and the easy sales were ended, the marijuana industry began taking its promotional operation more seriously, reinforcing its established markets and seeking to create new ones. Much of the credit of creating new markets for marijuana was attributed to Marty Soho, president of Soho-Kenhardt, known as one of the hottest creative ad shops in the business.

It was Soho who introduced the element of dignity and authority in marijuana advertising by bringing back doctors' testimonials. Soho, who in the late Sixties had created the "Hearing Mavin" character for a hi-fi account, reasoned that a similar touch of "expert opinion" would work for pot. And it did. Soho worked up an advertising presentation for Cheshire-feels built on film clips from the old "Marcus Welby, M.D." television series, and sold everybody everything.

The medical profession was delighted. In the old advertising days, doctors had earned bundles of money through endorsements. They appeared regularly in testimonial ads which ran in LIFE or LOOK or THE SATURDAY EVENING POST, reassuringly attesting to the cigarette's mildness, its flavor or its lack of irritation to the throat.

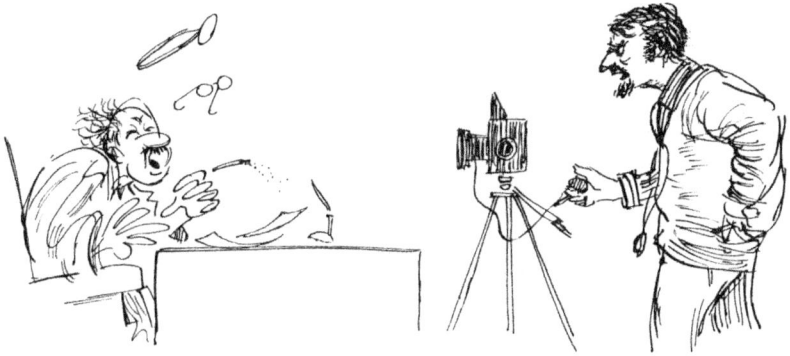

"C'mon, Dr. Lavin, hold still. Can't you stop coughing for even 1/250th of a second?"

Others, less photogenic could receive a handsome fee by merely allowing themselves to be counted in the ads which began, "more doctors smoke . . ." or "in a recent survey conducted among 300 leading physicians. . . ."

With the publication of the Surgeon General's reports, though, medical claims became obsolete and doctors were phased out of the advertising picture.

A few determined M.D.'s were still able to pick up a healthy dollar by publishing studies that either proved or disproved a causal relationship between cigarette smoking and cancer. Others, trying to stay "with it" during the years following, were sometimes able to transpose those studies to marijuana, reporting that pot smoking was (or on some rare occasions, was *not*) damaging to the brain, addictive, or whatever else was called for, but none of this amounted to anything financially significant.

*"Well, how about if I do
a study correlating marijuana use
with dandruff? . . . bad breath? . . . lint?"*

The advent of legal marijuana however, and Soho's promotional genius, created a new physicians' windfall. Doctors returned to the testimonial business with great zeal, endorsing, for fancy fees, all marijuana products. They also often prescribed specific pot products for their patients as effective, enjoyable tranquilizers, "for relief from common tension . . . and the quieting of jangling nerves," a practice which opened up lucrative financial tie-in possibilities with the drug manufacturers.

The more enterprising doctors did exceedingly well. A good case study is Dr. RX. This physician was a larynx specialist who, in the early Seventies, had visited China, and cashed in big on the acupuncture craze by working up a ventriloquist act with needles, which he performed on television and in Las Vegas. Dr. RX was even more successful with pot. Through well-placed interviews he promoted himself as having been "in" on the Mammoth Cave Project (actually, he did visit the caves once, on a Greyhound sightseeing tour), which gave him the aura of being even more authoritative than other doctors. This naturally justified his charging higher fees not only to the advertising agencies for his testimonials but to the few patients he had time for (who, being more or less voiceless, couldn't argue with him anyhow). Riding the sound wave of success, Dr. RX then became a silent partner in the development of an inhaler called *Smhighl*, which he endorsed in all its advertisements, plugged in all his books and articles, television appearances and nightclub acts,

*"Inhale away
your troubles
From your old
'toke bag.'
With Smhighl . . .
Smhighl . . .
Smhighl . . ."*

and, of course, prescribed to all his patients. The crowning
of his extraordinary achievements was his receiving a
telephone call from ex-President Nixon, congratulating him
on the announcement by the U.S. Chamber of Commerce
that Dr. RX's earnings for the year topped those of any other
doctor on the promotion circuit.

VI. Conversion of the Masses

Although the marijuana manufacturers were counting on increasing consumption among veteran users, they were more interested in converting the people who had never turned on before. It was Marty Soho, again, who devised the approach for "marijuananizing the masses," as he put it.

Soho assumed that most of the pot virgins were Middle Americans, the group which had once been identified by ex-President Nixon as his "New Majority." One of the group's more noticeable characteristics was its apparent preference for doing things in public which once had been considered private. Sex, for example. The widespread wife-swapping practices of the early Seventies were established as a largely Middle American function. Or deep interpersonal relationships, as in the case of a ten-week national television series called, "An American Family," which chronicled, in relentless intimacy, the gradual deterioration and breakdown of a real-life California family.

Marijuana fit the same syndrome, concluded Soho; it was just one more private experience going public. And so he reached out for the vast mass Middle American market through the massest medium of all—a prime-time television game show. The show was called, "The Pot's Right," and it was one of the biggest successes in television history, according to Marvin Kitman, the noted syndicated television critic. "The Pot's Right" brought together two pot-virgin couples and turned them on for the first time, in front of a studio audience and about 100 million other people. Sponsored by Cheshirefeels and Smhighls, it was basically a public-relation puff in a game-show rap. In general, it aimed for hysteria and screaming laughter (assured by a laugh track to fill in the studio audience's periodic stony silences) to demonstrate to the millions of viewers just how much fun marijuana could be.

All the shows were taped in advance, and the unforeseen downers edited out. Occasionally, the guests' sex impulses, liberated and magnified by turning on, produced some wild on-stage orgies. These were not televised, either, although they did provide extra viewing pleasure for the studio audience. Naturally, the reports of these "bonus happenings" were leaked to the right publicity sources, which guaranteed an SRO house for every taping, kept the show constantly in the national press, and helped it win top Nielsen ratings.

In structure, "The Pot's Right" somewhat resembled a poker game, played by two men and two women, and hosted by a Genial Potmaster, the veteran television emcee, Bill Howard. At the start, each player was given $200 with which to play. Taking turns, the contestants each pulled an envelope at random out of a large copper pot on stage. On the front of the envelope was written a subject category, like Travel, Sports, Music, etc., and inside the envelope was a statement about that subject, which was either "right" or "wrong." Bill Howard would announce the category and the player then bet that he would correctly tell whether or not the statement of the Pot was Right.

The other three players then made their bets, with him or against him. The first answering bet was made by the player's spouse, ostensibly to give the other couple some clue about the player's actual knowledge about the subject. Two raises were allowed. With the betting over and the Pot Right, the envelope was opened, the statement was read, and the player pronounced the Pot Right—or not. At the end of the show, the person with the most money won.

As a game alone, it could never have been a successful show, opined Mr. Kitman. But, as he saw it, "the game is merely a frame." The show actually began with Potmaster Howard turning the four players on with elaborate fanfare; colored spotlights, drum rolls, a blare of trumpets before each virgin drag of the Cheshirefeel or inhale of the Smhighl by the non-smokers, and plenty of studio-audience cheering. Through subsequent drags and inhales, to the accompaniment of a continual fire-engine version of "A Pot Time In The Old Time Tonight" under mind-blinking strobe lights, Howard constantly reminded the contestants (and everybody else) how stoned they were quickly getting and how much fun they were having.

As Mr. Kitman described it, "The show's well-publicized hilarity springs from the unpredictable behavior of the guests, who, following instructions, try to concentrate very hard on playing the game. At this, they are superbly unsuccessful. Instead, they lose the flow of the game constantly, drifting off into their own streams of euphoria, antagonism, anxiety or eroticism, depending on whom they are relating to—to themselves, their spouses, or any of the other strangers of the moment."

The following is excerpted from a typical show:

> (The players on this particular show were George and Betty Benjamin from Cleveland, and Charles and Phyllis Mednick from Chicago, and were typical of all the couples, selected from postcards and interviews, to appear on "The Pot's Right."
>
> George Benjamin was a huge, beefy man with a ruddy complexion and close-cropped hair. His hands curved as if they held invisible footballs and his laugh could be felt as well as heard. He worked for the Allstate Insurance Company as an adjuster of automobile-accident claims. His wife, Betty, was dark-haired and very petite. She said she had majored in home economics at college, where she had also been a cheer-

leader. The Benjamins had three boys and one girl, aged 15 to 4. Whenever Betty spoke, she giggled.

Charles Mednick was of medium height, smiling and round-faced, with a thin blond moustache and a retreating hairline. He looked well-scrubbed and well-groomed and his voice was musical, in a slightly nasal way. He worked for the Regal Paper Company, selling paper to printers, art studios, advertising agencies and the like.

Phyllis Mednick was a tall, large-boned woman with brown hair which hung straight down alongside her face. She was a librarian, she emphasized firmly, at the local high school. They had one child, a daughter of eleven.)

(EXCERPTS FROM TRANSCRIPTS,
POTS RIGHT/BA#74586-PT)

BILL: EXOTIC FOODS! Hear that, everybody—EXOTIC FOODS! George's subject is EXOTIC FOODS! How much are you going to bet, George?

GEORGE: (humming) Mmm-mm-mmm-mm mm.

BILL: George?

GEORGE: (singing) . . . *gim*-me what I cry-for, you know you got the kind of bo-dy that I'd—

BILL: Hi! Hi! George is high! See George high, everybody? George, listen to me and pay attention. George, hold it, pass that joint over to Phyllis; you're supposed to share it.

GEORGE: Oooooh-*oooooooooh!* Would I ever share my joint with Phyllis! Hot damn, but I feel horny! (studio audience screaming)

PHYLLIS: Please, Mr. Benjamin, you're *sitting* on me.

BILL: Come on now, George, sit back down in your own chair—that's it—and tell us—sit up, George—how much do you want to bet if THE POT'S RIGHT about EXOTIC FOODS?

BETTY: (giggling) Oh, that's silly. George doesn't know anything about exotic food.

GEORGE: How about exotic joints? Whaddya say, Betz, wanna share my joint?

BETTY: GEORGE! You're tickling—me! Joint? Isn't that the *silliest* word you ever—Joint!—Joint!—HEY GIMME A *J!*

GEORGE AND BETTY: *J!*

BETTY: GIMME AN *O!*

GEORGE, BETTY AND BILL: *O!*

BETTY: GIMME AN *I!* AY AY AY!

GEORGE, BETTY, BILL AND CHARLES: *AY AY AY!*

BETTY: Joint. Joint joint jointjointjointjoi—(studio audience screaming)

BILL: How about that, ladies and gentlemen! Isn't this positively hilarious? (studio audience applause) And remember, it's all brought about by POT! Yes, America, you can't ever go *wrong* with pot *beeee-cauuuse*—NOW LET'S HEAR IT, STUDIO AUDIENCE—*beee-cause*—THE POT'S RIGHT! (studio audience screaming and applause)

BETTY: —ointjointjointjointjointjointjoi—

* * * * *

BILL: All right, Charles, the bet is up to you. George wagered $50 that he *can* tell if THE POT'S RIGHT about exotic food, and Betty here, no, no, Betty, *please* take your hand away. Betty here bet $75 that he *cannot* tell. What do *you* think?

CHARLES: (dreamily: Mmmmmmmmm. I think—it's—sen—sation—al. I really feel fan—tas—tic. I mean, I can't act—ually—um—*smell* that envelope—from way over here—

BILL: WONDERFUL, Charles, simply WONDERFUL Hear THAT, everybody? He even SMELLS better! That's the power of pot, for you! Wonderful, Charles! Now, what's your bet?

CHARLES: (sniffing) Mmmmmm. I bet that envelope in your hand—is a 20-pound—80 percent rag-content bond—with a zinc sulphide filler—and—mmmm—a cockle finish—

79

BETTY: Cockle Finish. Cockle finish. cocklefinishcock-lefinishcocklefin—

BILL: What about THAT, ladies and gentlemen! Let's have a big round of applause for Charles Mednick! Charles Med (studio audience applause) nick, ladies and gentlemen!

CHARLES: Mmmm—and where is that luscious *vellum* I smell—?

* * * * *

PHYLLIS: I'm sorry to be such a poor subject, Mr. Howard, but I don't feel a thing. It seems apparent that these—uh—reefers are not affecting me one iota.

BILL: Now don't worry, Phyllis, you're doing fine; just fine, indeed. As a matter of fact, you're finer than you think—WOULDN'T YOU SAY, STUDIO AUDIENCE?—(studio audience applause) so just relax and make your bet.

BETTY: I-o-ta. I-o-ta. Iotailotaiotailotailotailotaiotaio—

PHYLLIS: If you say so, Mr. Howard. Well, in my opin-ion—Mr. Howard, would it be all right if I took off my shoes?

BILL: Of course, of course.

PHYLLIS: Thank you . . . . Oh—um—in my opinion, I very much doubt whether Mr. Benjamin has any knowledge whatsoever of exotic foods. I assume we're speaking of dishes like *canard à l'orange,* or Chinese waterchestnut stuffing—and so—

GEORGE: I'd know about stuffing *you,* baby. (studio audience screaming).

PHYLLIS: Oh, *really,* Mr. Benjamin.

GEORGE: Really, really really! How'd you like a big, exotic banana up—

BILL: GEORGE! ! ! (studio audience screaming) Sit back down and let Phyllis make her bet. Go ahead, Phyllis—

BETTY: —anabananabanana. Iotaiotaiota. IotaBanana. Io-tabananaiotabananaiotabanana. I *eat* a banana. I eatabanana Ieatabanana I eatabanana Ieatabanana Ieata—

GEORGE: Whaddya say, Betz, let's (BLEEP) (studio audience screaming).

PHYLLIS: Mr. Howard, would you mind terribly if I un-buttoned my blouse a bit?

BILL: Not at all. That's what happens, you know—"A little pot, and soon hot."

PHYLLIS: Aha! William Shakespeare. *The Taming of the Shrew.* Act IV, Scene i, line 6.

BILL : Right you are, Phyllis! Right—you—are! Let's hear it for her, folks.

(studio audience applause)

* * * * *

BILL: All right, now—everybody's bet is in and, George, it looks like nobody thinks you know much about exotic food.

GEORGE: Ahhhh, who gives a (BLEEP).

BILL: Well, um, anyway, the bets are in and THE POT'S RIGHT and we can get to the question. George, hand me the envelope, will you please?

CHARLES: Mmmmmm. Perhaps—with that 80 percent rag and zinc sulphide—a tiny touch of titanium oxide filler—

PHYLLIS: My, it's so warm in here. I wish I could—un-derstand why I—of all people—am not—experiencing any-thing at all—from—um—thi—um,—mari—wee—nie—

BETTY: Tit-anium. Iota titanium. titaniumiota titanium titanium tit—

GEORGE: She's got terrific titaniums, know what I mean? (studio audience screaming).

BILL: George—

GEORGE: Oh, baby, are you built and I mean, *built!* Oh, Phyllis, what jugs you—

(studio audience screaming).

BILL: Hold it, Phyllis! You can't take off any more clothing on the show. Phyllis, please, you'll have to—

PHYLLIS: This movement is an arabesque from—The Dance of the Hours—from *Les Contes d'Hoffman*—by Jacques Offenbach—

BILL: Thank you, Phyllis, thank you, that's enough now. Ladies and gentlemen, wasn't that absolutely fabulous? How about a big hand for Phyllis?

(studio audience applause).

GEORGE: How about *two* big hands for Phyllis? Oooooh, aaaahhhhh, just—one lit-tle squeeeeeeeeeze—

BILL: No, no, George—come back—PHYLLIS *NO!* You've got to leave that *on!*

(studio audience screaming).

BETTY: Tits. tits titstitstitstits. Iota tits iota tits. Iota *have* tits. Iota *have* tits. I—ota *haaaaaaaaaaave* tits.

CHARLES: Once—I sold some beautiful—65-pound purple cover stock—with a laid finish—to a sales-promotion agency that was doing a mailing piece—for PLAYBOY—

GEORGE: Ooooh, that's what I want—a beautiful piece from PLAYBOY—

BILL: Let's get back to the game, everybody. Pay attention now, George, here's the—George, are you listening?—here's the question: *"Sushi is an exotic dish from Japan."* Got it? OK, now, George, tell me, for $50, whether or not — THE POT'S RIGHT!

GEORGE: Mmmmmmm.

BILL: George? Sushi—

GEORGE: Sushi. Su-shi. Sushi? Ohhhhhhhh—if you knew—(singing) Su-shi—like I know—Sush—oh, oh! Oh, what a dish—

(studio audience screaming).

BILL: Now how about THAT, ladies and gentlemen. How about THAT! Is the man right or is he right! THE POT'S RIGHT! THE POT'S RIGHT! Wait, George, Leave Phyllis alone! Stop! George, Stop!

GEORGE: —so classy—as her—sweet—assy.

PHYLLIS: Ah! *Oui! Oui,* Jacques, *oui! Faites-moi!* Jacques, yes! Do me! Do me! doo-me doo-me doo-me doo-me—

(studio audience screaming).

BETTY: —doo-*me*—doo-*me*—doo-*me*—doo-*me* HEY! GIMME A DOO!

BETTY AND AUDIENCE: *DOOOOO!*

BETTY: GIMME A MEEEEEEEE!

BETTY AND AUDIENCE: *MEEEEEEEEEEEEEE!*

BILL: Betty, please! Keep your hands away fr—

BETTY! (music up, "Pot Time In The Old Town Tonight")

CHARLES: —then again—if I'd really been on my toes—I would have sold them an—mmm—antique finish with a deckled edge—

VII. A Country Gone To Pot

And so, thanks to Legalization, the entire United States of America finally was turned on. With the great majority of people using marijuana regularly, there was a basic change in the national temperament. Generally, people were calmer, more pleasant and less inclined to be hostile as they reacted to the normal problems of civilized living.

For those who worked at unstimulating jobs, pot made it easier and more fun to get through the day. Although it was true that the gross national product dropped off somewhat, so, too, did the rates of unemployment and on-the-job dissatisfaction. What was produced was apparently produced well enough, since consumer complaints dropped off also.

Other people, who worked in high-pressure situations, under constant strain and tensions, suffered from fewer heart attacks, migraine headaches and gastritis. Husbands, wives and children began enjoying each others company much more, practicing the popular new homily: "The family that 'highs' together, 'hi's' together."

But for all intents and purposes, the ordinary routines of day to day life continued pretty much the same as they had in the past—except for a slightly different twist here and there.

"Nothing to drink for us, thanks—for an appetizer, we'll turn on, then clams on the half-shell, then cream of celery soup, then . . ."

"—I had it for lunch."

*"Hey, buddy—can you spare some change
for a real good high?"*

*"Why not surprise her with one of our
103 flavors of marijuana drops!"*

*"Now **that's** a Welcome Wagon!"*

"Somebody must have turned on the computer—all it keeps saying is, 'Twas brillig and the slithy toves' . . ."

"It certainly does take the 'bored' out of board meetings. . . ."

VIII. The Attack On Pot

As might have been expected, though, the national feelings of satisfaction and well-being brought about by widespread pot were short-lived. Nor was it very surprising that the principal "snakes in our grass," as Raleigh Winnston called them, were the military/industrial complex and the liquor industry.

These groups had bitterly fought against Legalization from the very beginning because they feared that popular pot use would effectively ruin them. And they were right. As had been noted very quickly, with most of the country turning on, there was a definite decrease in manifestations of hostility and aggression. For the most part, people simply didn't rage and scream at one another the way they used to.

"Goodness! **This** phone is out of order, too!
That makes eight in a row! Oh, I feel so sorry for
the poor, suffering telephone company. . . ."

"Oh! Sorry, fella."   "No sweat, Mac."

"Oh, George, never mind the traffic report. . . .
Why can't you simply turn yourself on in the
morning, like other men do?"

Crimes of violence tapered off. Fighting phased out. Overt anger slumped. Which meant that if the trend continued to its ultimate conclusion, there would be no more wars. And if there were no more wars, then the weapons manufacturers would be out of business, to say nothing of the military itself becoming obsolete.

"Sergeant, take that man's name!"

A similar fate seemed in store for the liquor industry. As a matter of fact, complained one leading retailer, Fate was all that was in his store. His customers virtually disappeared as the country used pot more and drank less, Turning on had proven to be a better, safer way to relax than using alcohol. The advertising campaigns for pot had attacked liquor hard.

"Use Marijuana—No Hangover, No Habit!" cried the advertisements, citing the old Drug Commission studies which showed alcohol as the country's leading narcotic, a major disease and an oft-time contributing cause of death. "Better High Than Die," they trumpeted. "Better 'ON' Than 'GONE.'"

REACH FOR THE HIGH LIFE INSTEAD OF THE LOW-LIFE ...

© COUNCIL FOR MARIJUANA

If these arguments weren't strong enough, the clincher was that marijuana—in its various forms of cigarettes, candy, gum, inhalers and assorted other drug products—was much less expensive than any whiskey or beer. The military, industrial and liquor communities sought to halt the trend that threatened their existence. The liquor industry tried to organize a new lobby for the repeal of Legalization, called STTOP (the Society To Terminate Overt Pot). The military planned a new recruitment approach based on the philosophy, "You're not a *real* man unless you kick somebody in the groin and kill him a lot!"

It didn't work. The guys just smiled and kept turning (on) the other cheek.

Then one day, Mr. Shaefer Brumley, president of Brumley's Beer, formerly of Brooklyn before he closed down the 132-year-old plant to relocate in a more tax-sheltered area, looked through some sales figures and connected two thoughts. Brumley noticed that the largest and most severe drops in beer sales occurred on military bases and towns.

"It's because they're taking pot more," he burped angrily. "Damn pot! It fucks me up, it fucks up the army!" And he took another swig of beer.

That afternoon, General Grant Hackitt, head of the Joint Chiefs of Staff, received a phone call from Brumley. General Hackitt had just returned from a meeting with the Joint Chiefs at which they had voted unanimously to demand that Congress officially change the name of their group. Hackitt was desperate about the marijuana peril. He took Brumleys call without putting him on "hold."

"Hackitt here. What have you got, Brumley?"

"Hiyuh, Grant, how the hell are you?"

"Never mind the social amenities, Brumley. Consider that an order. Why did you call? Reee-port!"

"Hold it, Grant! Don't pull that bullshit on me; we're not even in the same pecking order!"

"Sorry, Shaefer. It's just that I'm under *great* pressure. Pshhhhhhhhhhhhhhhhhhhhhhhhhh! It's this pot peril! It's attacking our entire Armed Forces. The Armed Forces? Why, its undermining the Defense Department. And it's up to me, do you hear, to find a defense against it and so I tell you here and now that I cannot waste time listening to you whine about your miserable sales at the PX!"

"How the hell do you know that my sales are off at the PXs?"

"Oh, really, Shaefer, I *can* read, you know. The figures on those monthly checks I get from it you keep shrinking all the time."

"Oh, yeah, I forgot for a minute. But that's not what I called about."

"Well, I'm listening!"

"Grant, you and me have got to team up against pot."

"What do you mean?"

"What do you mean, what do I mean? I mean, gang up on it, shmuck, like in the old days. Together! Remember? We jump on it, kick it in the balls, beat the shit out of it— squoosh it bad! That fuckin' pot is ruining me, too, you know! The way things are going, I'll be out of business in six months. Listen, we've been trying on our own to—like you say—to come up with a good defense against the sonofabitch. But the best defense is a good offense! Right?"

"Hmmmmm."

"Remember 'attack'? Attack! Attack! Attack! Thats all you ever say, remember? So, we combine our forces and we *attack* pot. And maim the fucker for good! United we stand and all that. What do you say?"

"Ye-e-sssss. United we stand, divided we fall. Two if by land and one if by sea. Or is it—Right! I like it, Shaefer, it's not bad. It's even pretty good. But we can't attack without a plan. We must have a plan. A plan of attack, we call it in my line. We must—"

"Grant, it's all done. Meet me at seven at the Hilton bar and I'll lay out the whole works for you."

"Right. Roger, Shaefer, Wilco and Out."

"Yeah."

Shaefer Brumley's plan was enthusiastically embraced by General Hackitt. Their first move was to call in Harley Roardin of Defiant Motors, the most powerful automotive man in Detroit and all-time leading winner of defense contracts; and the plot against pot thickened considerably.

A few months later, a hardcore group of truck drivers loyal to the beer and liquor industry stood up at a meeting of the Teamsters' Union and spoke out for higher wages for delivering marijuana products.

". . . so let me make one thing perfectly clear—I say that this here marijuana—or pot— or whatever you want to call it—is a genuine menace! A dangerous threat to our lives. Why? I'll tell you why. Not because it maybe changes your head or messes up your genes like they say, because that don't mean shit anyway, but it's dangerous because it's real bad for the liquor business, which means the bread and butter in our pockets—or our mouths, however you want to call it—and that being the case, it represents a real and inherited threat and danger, and so if we got to handle this type of goddamn merchandise, then I say we gotta be paid a lot extra hazard pay for doing it!"

These men were supported by a group of longshoremen with similar loyalties and the union smoothly voted a request for a pay raise. The marijuana manufacturers had little choice but to agree to it. And reluctantly, soon afterwards, they raised the price of their marijuana cigarettes and drug products. It was the first of a long, continuing series of demands for pay increases by the Teamsters, followed by price increases on marijuana products.

At the same time, the military/industrial complex in Washington pressed hard for, and won, a new $300 billion allocation to develop an anti-retaliatory fourth-strike suburb-to-suburb missile. Congress was also persuaded that the funds come not from the already appropriated Federal budget, but should be produced from higher sales taxes on the nation's newest industry, which had yet to contribute to national defense. The effect of the surtaxes on marijuana products pushed their retail prices up still higher.

While price pressures were being engineered, some physical problems popped up to undermine the pot production line. Factories were suddenly plagued by mechanical breakdowns which caused work stoppages. The breakdowns were inevitably traced to the failure of some small piece of equipment which had been supplied by a company specializing as a subcontractor to a large military/industrial firm. All of this resulted in shortages at the retail level.

In addition to all of these problems, the American market was then suddenly flooded by huge supplies of much less expensive, foreign marijuana imports from all over the world. The most important of the imports were Rifs (pronounced "Reefs") from Morocco, and the all-time popular favorite, Acapulco Gold, appearing for the first time ever in attractive, well-produced packages.

from Morocco

Rif

(Say "reef")

You must remember this ...

Importing the Rifs and Acapulco Gold was the *piece de resistance* of Shaefer Brumley's master plan, according to which Harley Roardin and his associates personally went to Mexico and Morocco where, employing the sophisticated tactics and experience of many corporate wars, they quietly bought into, then took control of, the previously passive marijuana interests.

(A darkened room, part of the penthouse suite, in a luxury hotel in Mexico City. Heavy red velvet drapes have been almost completely drawn in front of venetian blinds. Slim slivers of daylight lie in a row on the thick carpeting, providing the only illumination in the room. Behind a desk angled in one corner of the room sits HARLEY ROARDIN, making notes with a gold ballpoint pen on a yellow legal-size pad. The door opens and the sounds of a party wriggle in. MARTY enters, then closes the door, clipping off the sound with the neat click of the latch.)

ROARDIN: (does not look up, but continues to write) Anybody else, Marty?

MARTY: Just one, boss. Garcia. (He reaches inside a breast pocket with some effort, the tuxedo being too tight for his large body, and withdraws a crumpled yellow paper.) Pedro Adolfo Manuelo Garcia.

ROARDIN: Who is he?

MARTY: He owns all that land between, uh, (he reads with difficulty) Gua-da-la-ja-ra and, uh, Man-za-nillo. Banana plantations, mostly but lots of good grass.

ROARDIN: (looks up, then leans back in his chair, rubbing his lower lip thoughtfully.) Ah, yes—Garcia. He's the one who's been giving us a little trouble, hasn't he, Marty?

MARTY: (runs his palm over the back of his crew-cut) Right, boss. Sal and me, we made him a nice offer and he refused it. How could he refuse it? Fuckin' wetback! He oughtta go back to where he came from!

ROARDIN: (softly) Let us not be disrespectful, Marty. We should always show respect, even though others may do otherwise. Besides, this *is* where wetbacks come from. Have we seen everyone else?

MARTY: (refers to his paper) Yeah, everybody who you invited, showed: (checks them off) Menendez, "El Malo," the head of the local syndicate, the army general, Jiminez, the two governors from D. F. and Guanajuato, the Martinez brothers who own the factories, *their* ambassador, *our*

109

ambassador, Ramon Ortega, the labor guy, and that whole bunch of private growers.

ROARDIN: (smiles). Ah, the growers. Oh, they were beautiful, weren't they, Marty? The way they came in and draped those leis of marijuana leaves around my neck—and did their little Mexican Pot Dance.

MARTY: Yeah. Now that's showing respect, huh? Like they should. And they were really happy to take the money and sign, weren't they, boss?

ROARDIN: (lights a cigar) Yes, they were, Marty, as all the others were indeed glad to do business with us, once they knew what we would do to them—(laughs)—I mean, *for* them, in return. And I think our stubborn Señor Garcia will see things our way, too. Marty, go and ask him to come in, will you? (MARTY turns towards the door) Oh, and Marty, hang around, will you? You know—in case I need you.

MARTY: (laughs) Right, boss.

(MARTY opens the door and goes into the next room, where the party continues. Snatches of conversation in Spanish and English are heard. Mariachi singing. Clinking of glasses. A lusty laugh of machismo. ROARDIN sits at the desk, rotating the gold ballpoint pen between the fingers of one hand. The door is pushed open again and MARTY re-enters with GARCIA, a short, stout man with a small black moustache and long flared sideburns. He is wearing a white suit and holds a handkerchief with which he continually mops his perspiring face. His other hand clutches a drink and a toothpick skewering three Swedish meatballs. He grins broadly upon seeing ROARDIN, revealing one gold tooth on either side of his mouth. GARCIA steps into the room and, with a graceful flourish belying a man of his build, executes a deep bow.)

GARCIA: (expansively) *Muy buenos días, señor. MUY buenos días.*

ROARDIN: (wryly) You're overdoing it, Garcia.

GARCIA: (in mock affront) Señor! You do me great disservice! Surely I intend no offense.

ROARDIN: Close the door, Marty. (MARTY closes the door, then leans back against it, folding his arms across his chest.) I'm not so sure about that, Garcia. I'm getting disturbing vibrations from you.

GARCIA: (protesting) But, señor, I am *here*—at your party —at your invitation—to pay my respects.

ROARDIN: (leans forward) In a *white suit,* Garcia? When the invitation distinctly said *formal?*

GARCIA: (smiling a pasty smile) A thousand pardons, señor, but my tuxedo was in the cleaners. (He gulps down the three Swedish meatballs at once, and slowly withdraws the toothpick from his mouth, savoring each centimeter.) And a man of my—(he pats his stomach)—ah, *build*— finds it impossible to rent one.

ROARDIN: (flatly) You might just as well have come in serape, poncho and sombrero.

GARCIA: (his eyes narrowing) Are you trying to provoke me, señor?

ROARDIN: (shrugs) I wouldn't think of it, Garcia. (He twirls the pen for a moment.) But I am very curious as to why you *did* come here.

GARCIA: (smiling again) The food.

ROARDIN: What?

GARCIA: The food, señor. I came for the food.

ROARDIN: The—*food?*

GARCIA: (happily) Si, señor. The stuffed cabbage. (Smacks his lips loudly) *Sobre saliente.* Sweet and sour tongue. Ahhh. Chicken chow mein. Mmmmm. Salmon and hard-boiled egg canapes—

ROARDIN: Garcia—

GARCIA: —anchovies and salami. Ohhh, and your franks in their little blankets. *Qué cosa!* And the tuna fish with sliced pimento olives, herring in sour-cream sauce, caviar on

Ritz crackers, pizza, chopped—

ROARDIN: Cut it, Garcia! (He stands, places his hands flat on the desk and leans forward, his eyes cold and glittering.) That's enough! You've had your little fun, but now it's time to stop playing games, my friend.

GARCIA: (sullen) It is you, señor, who is the one playing the games. (He drains the rest of his drink and mops at his perspiring neck with the large handkerchief.) And I am not your friend.

ROARDIN: (sits in his chair again, keeping his hands folded on the desk.) You continue to make the same mistake, Garcia. That's too bad. We come down here and offer you a nice business proposition, which you refuse, with contempt. I forgive you that and invite you here to give you another chance to be friends and partners, but you insult me by showing up in a white suit and grubbing all my food. You think you're being smart, Garcia? That's not smart. Not smart at all. Isn't that right, Marty?

MARTY: (from the door) Not smart, boss. He's got no respect.

GARCIA: (exploding in anger) Respect? Why should I have respect? Because you speak big words? I am not so stupid not to know you want to steal my land. You think you can come here and push everybody around? But not this one. Not Garcia. Not Garcia *El Fuerte!* (And in a swift, sudden move which catches both ROARDIN and MARTY by surprise, GARCIA reaches into his pocket and pulls out a handful of small green chile plants, which he holds out on his palm.) *Mira! Chile verde!* This type of chile is so hot, people cannot even pick one up in their bare fingers *Mira!* (GARCIA tosses the entire handful of chiles into his mouth and chews slowly and elaborately, his eyes, remaining tearless, staring defiantly and triumphantly at ROARDIN. Finally he swallows, leaving a grin spread widely across his face.) You see? It is for this that I am called *El Fuerte*—and it is why I care nothing for your threats, and fear you not.

ROARDIN: (nods slowly) Garcia, I am impressed by your curious appetites, but I cannot waste any more time mincing words with you. You *will* sell us your land, under the original terms we offered you, which, in view of the circumstances, you will have to admit, is most generous of us. If, however, you *still* refuse, then it most probably will come to pass, that —your sister—(he looks over at MARTY)

MARTY: (refers to the yellow paper) Maria Teresa—

GARCIA: (staggered) *Maria Teresa!*

ROARDIN: (continues) —Maria Teresa, will—ahh—be— pressed into service at a model/studio/massage parlor in midtown New York City—

GARCIA: (falls into a chair, mopping his neck) *Mi hermana!*

ROARDIN: —where gringo perverts will scrawl "wetback" in indelible colored magic markers all over her nude young body—

GARCIA: (twisting in pain) No, no, señor—*por favor*—

ROARDIN: —and she will be made to live in a city-run welfare motel and treated as if she were a poor Puerto R—

GARCIA: (screams) *Basta! Por Dios!* Enough, señor! I will sell, I will sell, but do not do this, I beg of you!

ROARDIN: (softly) Calm yourself, Garcia. If you are my friend, this cannot happen. We will even protect your sister from that possibility. What else are friends for? Right, Marty?

MARTY: Right, boss. Long as they show respect.

ROARDIN: (stands up, smiling) Garcia, go with Marty, now, and take care of the little business details. (GARCIA morosely heaves himself to his feet. ROARDIN holds out his hand. GARCIA hesitates, then takes it and shakes it.) Go in peace, my friend. (GARCIA shuffles off toward the door) And when you're finished with all the paperwork, come back and enjoy some stuffed cabbage and—*OW!* (ROARDIN shouts and fans the air furiously with his right hand) Sonofabitch!

113

MARTY: (freezes in the act of opening the door) What's the matter, boss? You all right?

ROARDIN: (blowing on his hand) I don't know! All of a sudden my goddam hand started burning like hell! Damn! It feels like it's on fire!

GARCIA: (grins from the doorway) It is the juice from the *chile verde,* señor. I have told you it is strong. Stronger than you think. (He grins again, to himself, then exits. MARTY glances over at ROARDIN again, then follows GARCIA, closing the door behind him.)

ROARDIN: (remains standing behind his desk, alternately fanning his hand in the air and blowing on it) The sonofa-bitch wetback maimed me! Hackitt should give me a Purple Heart for this. Never mind, though—with this last contract in the bag, it spells *curtains* for American marijuana! (he stops fanning and looks up) Jeez! What a great line to end a scene with!

* * * * *

Roardin's entrepreneur efforts were equally successful in colonizing all the other target areas; Vietnam, Nepal, Afghanistan, Turkey and Morocco, although local practices and customs often put a different slant on the bargaining table.

"So, Mr. Roardin, Hassan and I—we are happy to join you in marijuana business. Make many people with little eyes. Very nice. You like to drink mint tea? I have. I give you. Very nice. All Moroccan people drink mint tea. Smoke hashish. Make beautiful rugs . . . like this one . . . you like? . . . or babouche slippers . . . like these ones . . . or djellabas . . . kaftans . . . or they carve beautiful box with writing from the Koran . . . all cedar wood . . . all make by hand by Berber people . . . all very beautiful . . . you like something? . . . you tell me . . . I make you good price. . . ."

The American enterprises were encouraged by the foreign governments, not only because of the great dollar profits they expected to realize but also because of the promise of generous military aid from the United States. General Hackitt was very pleased with himself for having added what he called "another irony to the fire" by specifying that the bulk of this military aid consist of the very missiles produced from the new surtaxes on American marijuana. With Roardin and Brumley expertly applying American production know-how, the foreign marijuana streamed into the United States in a torrent, completely saturating the domestic market.

Thus, the multi-pronged attack of increased labor costs, higher taxes, sabotaged production and the invasion of the foreign product hit American marijuana very hard. For the Brumley-Hackitt-Roardin team, though, the game plan was being executed perfectly, and their hopes for total victory in the near future soared up and up.

IX. The Defense of American Pot

Staggered by a sharp drop in sales, rising costs, and plunging ever deeper into the red, America's marijuana industry regrouped and began to fight back. Activist Ron Norton set aside his ideological differences with Raleigh Winnston and joined him in the struggle. Immediately they redoubled their pressure on Congress for legislation to impose higher tariffs on the imports, to effect cutbacks in the military expenditures (which domestic marijuana alone was now paying for) and for a rollback on Teamsters' wage increases. (Truck drivers were, by this point in time, earning an average of $1,132.87 a week, just for delivering American marijuana products.)

The battle lines in Congress were never before so sharply drawn. Congressmen were forced to take clear-cut stands (against their normal, innermost desires) either for or against American marijuana. One very old senator, renowned for his classic issue-straddling techniques, his nerves frayed by the unrelenting pressures put on him by a half-dozen warring lobbies, stood up one day and proposed Prohibition of Everything, but he was silenced hurriedly.

The tensions in the country built steadily, growing and focusing into a titanic, unprecedented, multi-billion-dollar, one-on-one struggle of vested interests, not unlike two giant gladiators wrestling each other in the center of a vast, empty battlefield.

"You should drop dead, you filthy
pervert addict pothead!"
"Rot in hell, you dirty drunken dog!"

America's tobacco and drug lobbies and all their allied groups were very powerful and persuasive, and, after several weeks of bitter political infighting on Capitol Hill, were able to effect a $200 billion cutback in military expenditures and a freeze on Teamster wages.

However, despite their best efforts, Winnston and his supporters could do little about their most serious danger of all—the invading foreign marijuana products. It all came down to this: If Acapulco Gold, Rifs and all the others could not be prevented from flowing into the country, they would destroy the American marijuana industry and, in the process, argued Winnston, negate all the efforts that had gone into bringing about Legalization.

Orderly legislative action and due legal process had proved to be effective only to a point. If anything more was to be done to save American pot, it would have to be accomplished through more direct measures.

"Turn . . . on . . . A-me-ri-cannnnnnn . . ."

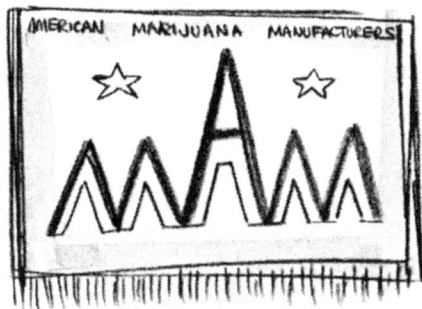

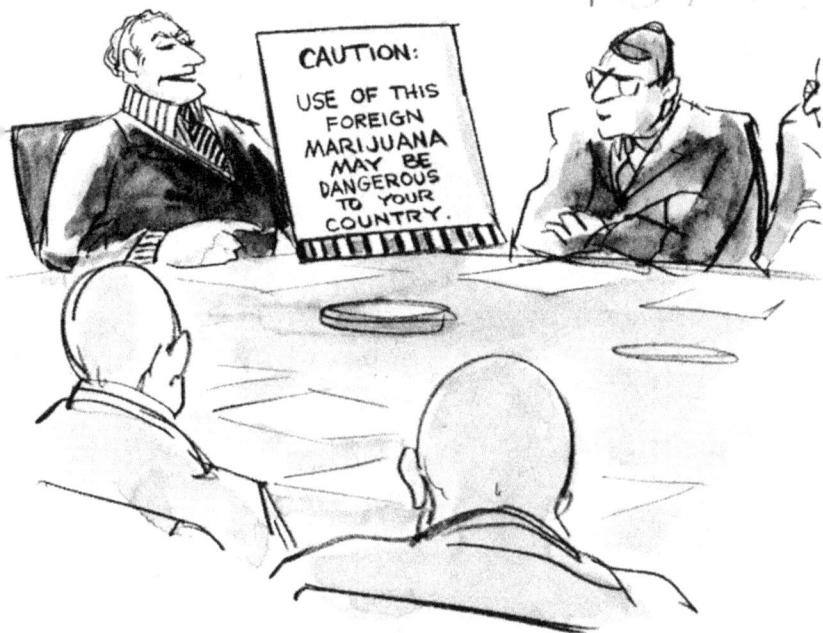

". . . we print up millions of tiny stickers, and paste em all over everything they make . . ."

*"In the old days, it was the Federales who'd
search you . . . now it's the
American Marijuana Manufacturers."*

In the back of a *cantina* named the "Cucaracha," in the town of Dolores Hidalgo, 198 miles north of Mexico City, five odd-looking men huddled around a small, knife-marked wooden table, conspiring.

The apparent leader of the group was a tall man dressed in an all-white cowboy suit, white hat, white boots and white gloves. He had driven into town in a white Rolls Royce with the name "Silver" stenciled on both front fenders. He wore a black mask and toyed continuously with a silver cigarette lighter shaped like a bullet.

Sitting next to him was a heavyset Mexican in wraparound sunglasses, with plump cheeks and a tiny moustache that peeped out between a bulbous nose and a pair of thick lips perpetually puckered up in the form of an *O*. He was wearing Pancho Gonzales-autographed tennis sneakers.

The other men at the table were disguised to conceal their identities. One wore a scuba-diving mask with a snorkel tube stuffing his mouth. Another had pulled a woman's silk stocking tightly over his head, contorting his face. The third was made up as a circus clown; white face, red tomato nose, wide grinning mouth, orange hair around the ears and an old Brooklyn Dodger baseball cap worn sideways on his head.

It was siesta time, and the silence and the thick, afternoon heat completely enveloped the group in the little room, sealing them off from the rest of the world. From a radio across the square, over the *jardin* thick with poinsettias, floated the solitary sound of a song; soft, rhythmic guitars insinuating their pulse under two tenor voices weeping in close harmony of *amor . . . alma . . . corazón. . . .*

The tall masked man shuffled through a pack of white, three-by-five cards which were filled with notes in shorthand, then turned to the heavy Mexican. "What do you say, Caballo," he said in a deep, resonant voice, "are we all here? Can we get this show on the road?"

Caballo's half-lidded eyes, behind his dark glasses, circled the table slowly. Two blinks per person. The Snorkel, the Stocking and the Clown blinked back.

"Si, señor," exhaled Caballo. "These are my men. *Estamos aquí.* I had also sent for a man from Vera Cruz but he does not yet come. Perhaps he could not find a disguise and so had fear that he would be noticed."

The masked man's jaw tightened and he pulled a package of Cheshirefeels out of his breast pocket and lit one with his silver bullet.

"Right." He grimaced as he spoke while trying at the same time not to exhale. "We . . . don't . . . want . . . to be . . . noticed . . . since . . . secrecy . . . izessentialtoour . . . Psssssssssssssshh-hhhhhhhhhhhhhhhh . . . needs!" And he exploded a cloud of pungent smoke, which filled the room and widened the eyes and nostrils of the others.

"Do not be concerned, señor. *Está bien,*" said Caballo, reaching for the pack of Cheshirefeels. "We can talk now and later I will tell the other of our plans."

"Fine, fine," nodded the masked man, I assume you've briefed these men about what they are supposed to do in their assigned areas, and given them the time schedules.

"Oh, *naturalmente,* señor," replied Caballo, lighting up a Cheshirefeel and passing the pack around to his companions.

"Good. I'd like to emphasize a few details and impress upon them the importance of this mission, so will you translate for me, Caballo?"

"*Como quiere.* As you wish, señor."

"Fine. All right, then, first of all, ask them if they fully understand what we want them to do."

"Si, señor." Caballo nodded and turned to the three men. "*Der Mensch mit dee shvartse Pawnim vawlt vaysen oyb Eer fahrshtayt yeder Zach vaws Veer vawlten,*" he said.

The Snorkel, the Stocking and the Clown nodded solemnly.

"Hey, wait a minute, what was all that?" demanded the masked man.

"Well, señor," explained Caballo, "when they shake their heads in that manner, it means that—"

"No, no! I mean, what language did you just talk to them in? It didn't sound like Spanish to me."

"Si, señor. It is not Spanish. It is Yiddish."

The Snorkel, the Stocking and the Clown nodded again.

"YEE-dish," affirmed the bobbing Snorkel, the word, muffled by the rubber mouthpiece, sounding as if it were spoken underwater.

"YEE-dish?" repeated the puzzled masked man, idly putting his silver-bullet lighter in his left ear. "Caballo," he said, his resonant voice now stern, "why do you speak to these men in YEE-dish?"

"Señor, it is so that you should not understand what we are saying.'

"*What?* What am I, *a child?*" pouted the miffed masked man.

"But, señor, you yourself have told us that everything must be done in secrecy. You yourself have given us the example with your cowboy suit. These men here are exceptional secret agents. Not only do they disguise their faces, but with language they disguise their tongues as well."

The Clown grinned and stuck out his tongue, which was painted a bright shade of Prussian blue.

The masked man recoiled. "I suppose you're right," he said uncertainly. "But tell me, Caballo . . . why YEE-dish?"

Caballo's eyes rounded, his lips pursed in the shape of a bagel, and his shoulders rose. "And why *not* Yiddish?" he answered.

The masked man shrugged back in capitulation, then turned to stare at the Stocking, who was sucking and inhaling noisily, struggling to get a deep drag on his Cheshirefeel through the silk stretched over his mouth. The Man in White looked back at Caballo, his eyes steely and probing.

"But just how could you know," he challenged, "that I myself do not speak YEE-dish?"

Caballo opened both palms outward. "Señor, did you ever know of a man in an all-white cowboy suit, driving a Rolls Royce named Silver, wearing a black mask and a silver bullet in his left ear, who spoke Yiddish?"

The masked man smoothed the wrinkles in his white gloves over his knuckles and nodded slowly.

"Very clever, Caballo," he said authoritatively. "All right, I think we can skip going over all the details again. Just remind your men that the timing of our operation is very important, that they should be certain to follow exactly the plans and schedules I gave them, and to remember that the fate of not only both our countries depends on them, but very possibly that of the entire free world of Western civilization as we know it."

"*Está bien,*" said Caballo, and turned to the trio, wagging his finger. "*Du hehrst? Machen dee Tseit zher goot!*"

The masked man frowned. "That was it? Caballo, it seems to me that a lot was lost in the translation, there."

"*Qué lástima,* señor; one must not cherish such high hopes from subtitles."

"Also, that sounded like pretty lousy YEEdish."

"I'm a Mexican secret agent, señor, not Golda Meir."

The masked man stood up and dropped the three-by-five cards into the heavy ceramic ashtray which sat on the table. "OK, Caballo, from here on it's your jai-a-lai game. You savve what I mean?"

He removed the silver bullet from his ear, flicked at it with a gloved thumb and touched the sudden flame to the index cards. "Now, you don't know me, you never met me, you never heard of me. And vice versa. Savve?"

The five men stared at the flame until it turned the white cards into black ashes. The masked man turned the ashtray over, spilling the ashes on the earthen floor, and ground them into dust with his heel. Then he straightened and strode sharply to the door, paused and turned.

"Break a leg, amigos," he said. And then he was gone.

There was a deep-throated roar from a powerful automobile engine, a screeching of tires and a hearty cry of "HIYO SILVER!" And seconds later, heavy silence again enveloped the room.

The Snorkel pulled his gaze away from the door and turned to face Caballo.

"Noo, Caballo," he asked, *"vehr iz der Meshuggener? Ehr iz, efsher der Lone Ranger?"*

Caballo picked up a piece of ash and slowly rubbed it out of existence between his palms. He looked toward the door with his sleepy eyes and shook his head.

"No," he said, *"—nisht der Lone Ranger, shmuck. Dass hombre vass*—Raleigh Winnston III.

"Carramba!" exclaimed the Stocking.

Funny, said the Clown, "—he didn't look it."

* * * * *

The next day, and during the week following, demonstrations were staged outside all the marijuana factories in Mexico, from the largest Acapulco Gold plant to the Smallest Potstillos factory. Thousands of men, women and children marched, protesting the existence in Mexico of the Yankee Capitalist Imperialist Exploiter, and threatening destruction and violence against all United States marijuana interests in Latin America.

The Mexican Government reacted only casually, attributing the disturbances to harmless Communist agitators, and, yawning, sent a small handful of troops to quell them. When news of the demonstrations reached Washington, however, General Hackitt correctly concluded that this was the work of the Winnston forces. He met with Brumley and Roardin, then acted quickly, and, through a series of swift phone calls and high-level meetings, Hackitt dispatched some American "military advisors" to support the Mexican Federales against the insurgents.

Some of the newspapers protested. "American troops do not belong on Mexican soil," they editorialized. Mothers cried out, "I didn't raise my son to die from dysentery." The American Society of Travel Agents filed a suit against the Government, charging restraint of trade. The Cubans called up the Russians on the red telephone and put them on "hold."

General Hackitt acknowledged the tenseness of the situation by appearing on television to explain the country's actions to the American people. He had convinced the President, said the General, that sending in American troops was "merely a precautionary measure . . . motivated solely by the desire to protect and honor our commitments to our beloved American interests in Mexico . . ."

*". . . and to demonstrate clearly, so
that there can be no mistake . . . that the
American Government will not tolerate
any vile attempt by Communists to undermine
and take over anything which we hold dear."*

Accordingly, he was also announcing that night that he was increasing the American buildup in Mexico, escalating our role from "passive advisor" to "active combatant" and that he had requested Air Force bomber pilots to include maps of the Mexican countryside (where the insurgents were concentrated) as part of their bedtime reading, along with John Wilcock's "Mexico on $5 a Day."

Raleigh Winnston and Ron Norton had been backed into a corner and they knew it. The Hackitt Brumley-Roardin forces had definitely committed themselves; they would stop at nothing to make sure that Acapulco Gold and all other foreign marijuana continued to flow, uninterrupted, into the United States and ruin them.

"Gentlemen, we have been backed into a corner and we know it."

"You're right, Raleigh. The Hackitt-Brumley-Roardin forces have definitely committed themselves; they will stop at nothing to make sure that Acapulco Gold and all other foreign marijuana continues to flow, uninterrupted, into the United States —and ruin us."

"Funny how that sounds so familiar, Marty."

"It's what we've all been thinking, Ron."

"Well, what do we do?"

"We have only one option left, gentlemen."

"You mean—?"

"Desperate situations call for desperate measures. They've got us over a barrel, up the creek, against the wall, by the short hairs. Time and metaphors are running out. Gentlemen, our joint is under attack. We *must* act. Are we agreed?"

"Agreed, agreed."

"Very well. Anselmo—you know what to do?"

"Si, *Kimosabe.*"

And so, early the next morning, every marijuana processing plant in Mexico (and in all other involved countries) was blown up. Blasted out of existence. Totally destroyed in one big bang, "Up in Smoke," ventured the Associated Press.

"Don't worry—maybe we come down mañana—or maybe the day after. . . ."

Raleigh Winnston's total destruction of the foreign marijuana industry shocked the entire world with its monumental daring. The United Nations held its collective breath for eleven consecutive hours following the explosions, anticipating with dread the retaliatory military action threatened by the United States—action which they well knew might plunge them all into another global holocaust.

The citizens of the world gnawed their knuckles in front of their television sets. And the American B-52 pilots sweated in their squadron rooms, coiled, taut with tension, half-expecting, half-fearing the *"go"* order.

It never came. The shoe was never dropped. In the final moment, General Hackitt was overruled by a Congress that had been pushed to the brink, but not quite over.

The bold Winnston's move was completely successful in breaking the foreign stranglehold on the American pot market. With the anti-pot coalition stunned and temporarily ineffective, the domestic manufacturers moved quickly to reinforce their political positions and set their production lines in high motion.

But Shaefer Brumley was not through, yet. Playing his last trump card with a vengeance, Brumley ordered his Teamster loyalists to strike, thus shutting off delivery of all American marijuana products, cigarettes and drug items alike, like a faucet turns off water.

The manufacturers stormed into Washington and screamed restraint of trade, Taft-Hartley, Robinson-Patman, Batman-Robin, everything they could, but they were helpless as the unions held fast. While the legal battles went on, the manufacturers tried to make deliveries themselves, but that caused too much violence at the picket lines. They also appealed to Congress to send in the National Guard to drive the trucks, but General Hackitt declared that this was neither a national emergency nor a disaster area, and convinced the President to refuse the request. With undelivered marijuana products piling up in the warehouses, the manufacturers slowed down their production. Pot was now merely trickling out to the public, and only through a few specialty stores, like Bonwit Teller and Saks Fifth Avenue, which could send buyers to the warehouses to pick up their own orders on the strength of sheer charm alone.

*"I mean it, Anita—I wouldn't call this
having enough pot to kiss on!"*

But this did not relieve the nationwide shortage. There were
no longer any foreign marijuana products on the market, and
American marijuana couldn't even get there to take advantage
of it. Production slowed down even more, and there were lay-
offs—of factory workers, sales personnel and (very quickly)
some high-priced talent at the big advertising agencies.

The legal wrestling continued, fiercely, on Capitol Hill, at high-level meetings and in lobbies all across the country.

But all the man on the street knew was that there was no marijuana at all—no more; and the very idea of commercial marijuana again seemed only like a dream—something long ago and far away—over the rainbow—someone else's high.

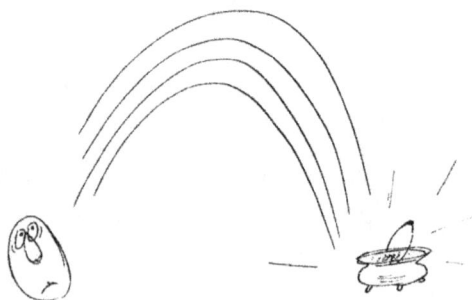

X. Restoring the Balance

An eerie feeling of disquiet draped over the nation like a winter afternoon during a partial eclipse of the sun.

Because there was less marijuana, people were turning on less. But it brought no smiles to Shaefer Brumley, for neither had they returned to drinking, as he had hoped. Soberly, quietly, the people began to think about how much they had been affected by what some philosophers of the day termed "forces outside the Self," and they looked for a new approach for themselves.

Because of the severe shortage of marijuana cigarettes, a joint had become a very rare and special item. When people would gather together, if one of them had a joint, everybody would share it. One person would take a puff, then pass it on to his neighbor, who would take a drag and pass it on to the next person, the process continuing until nothing was left except a tiny bit, which someone remembered was once called a "roach." Usually, the host or hostess would put the bit in a box, saving it with other "roaches" to make another whole joint—by hand.

It was all a very personal, intimate, communicating, sharing kind of experience, refreshing and uplifting. There were usually a few people in the crowd, old-timers mostly, who would recall with nostalgia that this was the way it Used To Be. That passing a joint around the room was the Good Old Way of turning on.

As the pot drought dragged on, more and more people had the opportunity to experience marijuana in the Good Old Way. Because all manufactured products were so scarce—and consequently so expensive—the old method of simply growing your own pot (without the camouflage, though) became popular again. The practice was extremely elementary and highly satisfying for everyone. Homegrown-pot parties were suddenly and breathlessly "discovered" by NEW YORK Magazine as "the innest, chic-est, kitchy-est thing, particularly among those who were anybody."

> Inevitably, a super-private pot club opened in Chicago, called *The Smoke-Easy*, where members would lie around a plush room, inhaling deeply sucking in great clouds of marijuana smoke blown in through the ventilating system. To insure exclusivity, customers could gain entrance only by knowing somebody, and the club itself was concealed inside a restaurant called, *The Blind Pig*, a nostalgic nod to the ancient days of Prohibition.

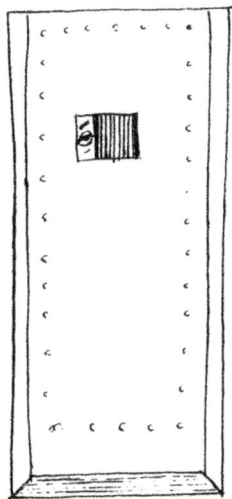

One knocked on a heavy door with a small, sliding window in the middle of it, which was "recessed an important two inches, so the guard can filter out undesirable elements" in the persons of actors who, during the course of an evening, assumed the roles of "narcs" threatening to "raid the joint."

The Smoke-Easy was very appealing, both from the standpoint of physical enjoyment as well as for a certain "philosophy of individual self-determinism" it seemed to represent, according to one noted sociologist.

Although many people were making adjustments to the continuing pot drought, Raleigh Winnston II was angry and frustrated. The court battles against the Teamsters' strike, the surtaxes, and other related issues which were combining to choke off marijuana business, were still unresolved, with no agreements in sight. Every day of the stalemate was costing his industry hundreds of thousands of dollars in expenses and lost profits. On top of that, reports of "do-it-yourself" pot practices were increasing and causing him additional concern.

Then one evening, it occurred to Winnston that during his own recent weeks of lobbying and fighting to "liberate commercial marijuana from American oppression," Ron Norton had been conspicuously absent from the battle. Where had the hero of Legalization been, wondered Winnston. What was he doing and why was he not in the middle of the action, when his talents and influence were so badly needed? Irritated, Winnston reached for the telephone and dialed Norton's number.

The phone was picked up after only one ring and Norton's voice came on the line.

"Hello. This is Ron Norton, talking to you on an automatic answering—"

"Shit!" muttered Winnston.

"—service machine. I'm out right now, but if you leave a message—"

"You sonofabitch!"

"—I'll call you back when I return. Wait until you hear the beep—"

"I bust my ass for pot and where is he? Probably out screwing around—him and his goddam tight-ass—"

"—before you start speaking. You will then have about twenty seconds for your message. Remember to wait until you hear the beep—"

"—high-and-mighty ways—keeping pot on some holier-than-thou level—"

"—and please be patient; it'll take a few seconds. Thank you for calling."

"—off in the clouds someplace, having nothing to do with reality—giving me all that noise about principles. Principles! Bullshit! *Money* is all the principles that count. You little bastard—you're costing me millions of dollars—Where The FUCK ARE Y—"

"BEEEEEEEEEEEEEEP"

"Oh—um—ah, HI, THERE, Ron-buddy! Long time, no talk! Raleigh Winnston here, Ron. Wanted to talk to you— naturally—heh-heh—um, call me back as soon as you can, eh? Thanks, buddy—um—beep-beep—heh-heh."

Ron Norton leaned forward and turned off the monitor on the telephone machine, through which he had just been listening in on Raleigh Winnston's entire call. "All that noise about principles" he repeated. "Oh, Raleigh Winnston, you never change." He pushed himself backwards in his chair, clasping his hands behind his head, and resumed staring up at an old poster on the Wall, advertising "Reefer Madness," the old film classic that proclaimed the evils of marijuana. Yessir, he thought, we've come a long way, Virginia, to get where we are today. . . .

A few days later, Ron Norton, hero of marijuana Legalization, held a press conference at which he announced his intentions to lead a backlash movement against commercial marijuana. He spoke of the "errors of excesses," citing "incessant, greedy advertising"; and constantly rising costs, which had made the price of pot more prohibitive to the user than any old law which had established it as illegal. He scored the manipulations and politicking that had nearly led to an incredible war with Mexico, our good neighbor to the south, and, in general, railed against the escalating exploitation of marijuana and how "a good thing seems to have gotten out of hand."

"In fact, this is another form of 'Reefer Madness,'" said Norton. "All this hysterical activity and battling over a simple pleasure? It's crazy! Through Legalization, all we ever wanted was the right to use marijuana however, wherever and whenever we wished. Whenever *we* wished. Not when somebody *else* wished. Just because its legal doesn't mean that you have to use it *all* the time!

"Like all those ads still trying to sell me Cheshirefeels—even though there aren't any in the stores now—pushing me to turn on more and more because they say it's *good* for me! Bullshit! Meaning really that it's good for Raleigh Winnston's business! Telling me to turn on just turns me off!"

Norton was asked how he felt about the continuing Teamster strike against the marijuana manufacturers and how he was helping to break it.

"I say, fuck it!" declared Norton. "And you may quote me, if you can!" Norton went on to say that manufactured marijuana was all too much trouble.

"I don't need commercially-produced pot to live. *Nobody* does. The only thing that's really important is that pot is now legal! Hell, I actually *enjoy* growing my own."

The story was plastered all over front pages and was a special
announcement that interrupted the regular telecast of "As
The World Turns On." NORTON NIXES COMMERCIAL
POT screamed one headline. NORTON SAYS TO TURN
YOURSELF ON, shouted another. On the television evening
network news, Norton was seen demonstrating his personal
technique for rolling a joint and for growing marijuana in a
wooden cream-cheese box on his window sill.

The nation looked and listened and nodded in agreement. "Right on," the people said. "Pot is for people, not profit." And within a week, Norton-assisted consumers' groups were leading countrywide demonstrations against what they called "unfair practices of the marijuana cigarette and drug manufacturers," demanding that they lower all prices, tone down their marketing activities to a minimum and, in general, conduct themselves with a good deal more moderation.

The new movement to "free pot" received heavy and enthusiastic media attention, and grass-roots support swelled. Raleigh Winnston's fury knew no bounds at first, but he realized fairly soon, as he had pre-Legalization, the wiseness of changing with the times; besides, there was the old adage about some profit being better than no profit at all.

And so, at a "joint heads of state" meeting among all the cigarette and drug manufacturers of marijuana, Winnston recommended that they all relax and agree to the demands of the people. Commercial marijuana would continue, "but nicely, now," according to the resolution, which was adopted unanimously.

The Teamsters interpreted the Marijuana Association action as removing that "threat of a present and inherited danger" to them, and they also relaxed, ended their strike and happily went back to work, admitting at last that marijuana had become a simple fact of life . . .

"I'd recommend the wheat—or, if
you're feeling particularly conservative,
buy the marijuana futures. . . ."

*"Her name is Marcia and she does **everything!**
She blinks, drinks, laughs,
wets her bed and gets high on pot."*

"Look there, Cynthia—in that field—there's some tickle-bellied, high headed, grin-faced **Cannabis sativa!"**

JACK AND JILL

Jack and Jill went up the hill.
To get a little high;
Jack came down and walked to town
But Jill stayed up in the sky.

"Did you see this special offer? For three
box tops and a quarter, you get
a combination secret-whistle-ring-and-
Roll-Your-Own-Joint outfit."

"Well, Judith, I guess now
we owe **them** a little trip. . . ."

. . . and that with the added touch of moderation, the process of Legalization had finally been concluded, to the satisfaction of everyone.

"OK, now here's Plan B . . ."

Well—*nearly* everyone.

About The Author

Mort Gerberg is a multi-genre cartoonist and author whose work has appeared widely in magazines, newspapers, books, online, television and home video. He is best-known for his cartoons in *The New Yorker* and for his book, "Cartooning: The Art and the Business."

For more, visit **mortgerberg.com**

You can also follow Mort on:
twitter.com/mortgerberg
facebook.com/mort.gerberg.7
instagram.com/mortgerberg/

Also recently re-released by Mort Gerberg

Right On, Sister!

Reaganworld